Things to Know before investing in an electric car charging station installer company

First published by Kjøller 2023

Table of Contents

Introduction

The electric car industry is rapidly growing, and with it, the demand for electric car charging stations increases as well. As a result, many companies have emerged as installers of these stations, each with its own unique set of terminologies, processes, and standards. As a potential investor, it's important to have a comprehensive understanding of the industry and the companies you are dealing with before making any investment decisions.

This glossary aims to provide you with the most commonly used terms and phrases when it comes to electric car charging station installers. It covers everything from the technical aspects of the installation process to the business models these companies use. With this knowledge, you will be better equipped to evaluate the potential of these companies and make informed investment decisions that offer both financial and societal benefits.

AC Charging

AC charging is the most common type of electric vehicle charging available. It uses the alternating current (AC) from a power source to charge the batteries in the vehicle. The charging station installer should provide high-quality AC charging systems that are compatible with a wide range of electric vehicle models.

Amperage

Amperage refers to the amount of electrical current that flows through an electric vehicle charging station. It is measured in amperes (Amps) and affects the speed at which the vehicle's batteries are charged. Higher amperage means faster charging times, but it also requires a higher capacity electrical supply. When investing in a charging station installer, it is important to consider the amperage that will best suit your charging needs.

Amp-Hour Rating

Amp-hour rating refers to the amount of electrical energy that can be stored in a battery. It is measured in amp-hours and affects the battery capacity and charging time. The charging station installer should have a thorough understanding of the amp-hour rating of the vehicle's batteries to ensure efficient charging and prevent overcharging or damage.

Anode

The anode is a component of an electric vehicle charging station that provides electrical current to the vehicle's batteries. It is the positively charged terminal that helps transfer electrons to the cathode, which is negatively charged. The anode is made of materials that can withstand the high voltage requirements of the electric vehicle charging process. It is important to choose a charging station installer that uses high-quality anodes that are durable and efficient.

App-Based Control

App-based control refers to the use of a mobile application to initiate and monitor the charging process. This feature is convenient for electric vehicle owners as it allows remote charging control without physical interaction with the charging station. A charging station installer that offers app-based control can enhance the user experience.

Area Requirements

Area requirements refer to the physical space needed to install an electric vehicle charging station. It includes factors such as the size of the charging station, its position, and safety regulations. Before investing in a charging station installer, it is important to ensure that the area requirements are met to ensure a safe and compliant installation.

Authentication

Authentication is the process used to verify the identity of the user and the vehicle before initiating the charging process. The charging station installer should have a secure authentication protocol in place to prevent unauthorized access or fraudulent use.

Automated Payment

Automated payment refers to the use of an electronic payment system to complete the charging transaction. The charging station installer should provide a secure and reliable automated payment system that is easy to use and accepts a range of payment methods.

Backup power supply

A backup generator or battery system that ensures the car charging stations continue to operate during power outages. It is an essential feature that provides a reliable service to clients and ensures minimal downtime.

Bid

This is a proposal submitted by an electric car charging station installer company to a client. It outlines the scope of work, timeline, and estimated cost. Before finalizing, it is wise to review multiple bids to compare price, timeline, and quality of services being offered.

Billing and payment policies

Guidelines outlining how the electric car charging station installer company will charge clients and process payments. These policies should be transparent and straightforward, including cost breakdowns, payment due dates, and acceptable payment methods.

Branding

The process of building a brand's identity through creative visuals, messaging, and marketing that represent its values, goals, and mission. A strong brand can differentiate the electric car charging station installer company from competitors, attract more clients, and ensure customer loyalty.

Building codes

Local or state regulations that outline specific requirements for installing electric car charging stations. Electric car charging station installer company needs to be aware of and follow building codes to ensure their installations are safe and compliant with regulations.

Building permits

Legal permits required by local or state authorities to build or install electric car charging stations on private or public properties. The electric car charging station installer company must obtain the required permits before starting installation to verify compliance with government regulations.

Business insurance

Insurance coverage that protects the electric car charging station installer company against damages, legal claims, and other risks. It is essential to select adequate coverage that includes liability, property damage, and workers' compensation.

Business license

A legal document required to operate the electric car charging station installer company. It is issued by the relevant government agency or authority and verifies that the company has met all necessary legal and regulatory requirements to provide services in a specific location.

Business plan

A comprehensive document that outlines the goals, strategies, marketing plans, and financial projections of a business. Before investing in an electric car charging station installer company, it is crucial to review their business plan to ensure they have a solid foundation and growth plan in place. The business plan should give you an indication of how the company plans to expand, the target market, and how it will generate revenue.

Certification

Certification refers to an installer's accreditation and compliance with industry standards and regulations. When investing in an electric car charging station installer company, it's imperative to ensure that they are certified installers. A certified installer ensures that the charging stations meet the required regulatory standards and will work efficiently without any issues or damage to your car.

Charging station compatibility

Compatibility refers to the ability of a charging station to work with a particular electric car's charging requirements. Before investing in an electric car charging station installer company, it is essential to ensure that they are installing charging stations that are compatible with your electric car. Compatibility is determined by the type of charging connector used by the charging station and the electric car. The charging rates, voltage, and amperage also impact the compatibility of the charging station with your electric car.

Charging station installation time

Installation time refers to the duration it takes to install a charging station in your home or business. The installation time varies depending on factors such as the type of charging station, location, and permits required. When investing in an electric car charging station installer company, understand the installation time required and plan accordingly.

Charging station location

Location refers to the physical location of the charging station, where it's installed. When investing in an electric car charging station installer company, you need to choose the most convenient location for the charging station. Factors such as accessibility, distance from your home or business, security, and the available power supply can impact the location choice.

Charging station maintenance

Maintaining a charging station is critical to ensure it works efficiently, lasts long, and is safe to use. When investing in an electric car charging station installer company, ensure that they provide maintenance services to keep your charging station in good condition. A maintenance routine could include checking the charging cords and connectors, inspecting the electrical panels, and removing any debris or buildup around the charging station.

Charging station network

A charging station network is a group of charging stations that are owned and operated by a single entity. When investing in an electric car charging station installer company, it is essential to understand what charging station network they are using. Some popular charging station networks in the USA include Tesla's supercharger network, ChargePoint network, and EVgo network. Before investing in a charging station installer company, ensure that they have experience working with the charging network that suits your electric car.

Charging station providers

Charging station providers refer to the entities responsible for owning and operating the charging stations. When investing in an electric car charging station installer company, understand who the charging station providers in your locality are. It's essential to choose an installer with experience in working with various charging station providers to ensure compatibility and a smooth installation process.

Charging station type

There are two types of charging stations for electric cars

Cost

The cost of installing an electric car charging station varies depending on factors such as the charging rate, type of charging station, and location. When investing in an electric car charging station installer company, ensure that they provide an accurate estimate of the cost involved in installing a charging station, including the installation cost, any permits required, and upkeep cost.

Customization

Customization refers to the flexibility to make changes to the charging station's design, placement, or features to suit your needs. When investing in an electric car charging station installer company, ensure that they provide flexibility or options to make changes based on your requirements. Customization often requires additional costs, so ensure you discuss these with the installer before the installation process.

Data Analysis

Data analysis involves the gathering and processing of data to generate meaningful insights that can inform decision-making. Before investing in an Electric Car Charging Station Installer Company, it is important to consider their proficiency in data analysis. This will help you understand how they gather and interpret data, which is critical to the efficient and effective installation of charging stations. A company with a proven track record of successful data analysis will be better equipped to handle any unexpected challenges that may arise during the installation process.

Deployment

Deployment refers to the process of installing and commissioning the charging station, including configuring, testing, and training. A successful Electric Car Charging Station Installer Company must have a skilled deployment team that can handle every aspect of the deployment process. They must be able to complete the deployment quickly, efficiently, and on budget, with minimum disruption to their customers.

Design

Design refers to the creation of a plan or blueprint that outlines the scope, features, and functionality of the charging station. A good Electric Car Charging Station Installer Company should have a strong design team that can create innovative and cost-effective solutions tailored to your specific needs. A well-designed charging station will be more efficient, reliable, and user-friendly, improving customer satisfaction and increasing revenue.

Development

Development refers to the process of continuous improvement of the company's processes, products, and services. A progressive Electric Car Charging Station Installer Company must have a development team that focuses on research and development to create innovative solutions, improve efficiency, reduce costs, and enhance the customer experience. A continuous process of development will help the company remain competitive in the increasingly dynamic automotive industry.

Diagnostic Tools

Diagnostic tools refer to the software and hardware tools used to diagnose any problems with the charging stations. A good Electric Car Charging Station Installer Company must have a comprehensive set of diagnostic tools and be proficient in their use. This will allow them to quickly identify and resolve any issues that may arise, reducing downtime and improving the customer experience.

Distribution

Distribution refers to the process of delivering the charging stations to their intended locations. A competent Electric Car Charging Station Installer Company must have an efficient distribution network that can ensure timely and cost-effective deliveries. The distribution process must also take into account the transportation requirements and restrictions imposed by local authorities and regulations for electric vehicles.

Diversity

Diversity refers to the range of services offered by the Electric Car Charging Station Installer Company. A company that offers a diverse range of services, such as installation, maintenance, repairs, and upgrades, will be better equipped to handle any issues that may arise throughout the lifespan of the charging station. This will ensure maximum uptime, reduce costs, and provide a better return on investment.

Documentation

Documentation refers to the creation and maintenance of all necessary records to ensure compliance with regulatory authorities and administrative purposes. A good Electric Car Charging Station Installer Company should maintain accurate, detailed documentation for all their installations, including permits, approvals, contracts, and warranty information. This will help simplify any future maintenance or repair work and reduce potential legal risks.

Durability

The durability of the charging station is an essential consideration when investing in an Electric Car Charging Station Installer Company. The charging station should be built to withstand harsh weather conditions, potential vandalism, or accidents. A well-built charging station should last for many years, require minimal maintenance and repairs, and deliver maximum uptime.

Electric Code Compliance

An electric vehicle charging station installer company must comply with local, state, and national electrical codes and regulations. Compliance includes adhering to the National Electric Code (NEC), National Electrical Installation Standard (NEIS), and The Institute of Electrical and Electronics Engineers (IEEE) 1547 standard, among others. Electric Code Compliance ensures the safety and reliability of electric vehicle charging stations.

Electric Grid Integration

Electric Grid Integration is a process that enables the integration of the distributed generation of electricity into the electrical grid to provide optimal electricity generation, transmission, and distribution. A charging station installer needs to be well-equipped with knowledge related to grid integration, including the types of interconnection equipment, such as inverters, smart chargers, and frequency regulation.

Electric Vehicle Supply Equipment (EVSE)

Electric Vehicle Supply Equipment (EVSE) is the infrastructure that supplies electric energy for recharging plug-in electric vehicles (PEVs) via electric-powered charging stations. EVSE can be used for both residential and public charging stations. There are two types of chargers, Level 1 (120-volt) and Level 2 (240-volt), with Level 2 being the most common in commercial settings. If you're considering investing in an electric car charging station installer company, you must be familiar with EVSE as it is the essence of electric vehicle charging.

Electrical Design

Electrical design is the process of planning and designing electrical circuits, systems, and equipment. In the electric car charging station installer company, an electrical designer is responsible for designing and integrating electrical components and systems to ensure that charging stations meet local state and federal regulations. That includes evaluating loads, providing circuit layout drawing, and planning electrical distribution systems.

Electrical Engineering

Electrical engineering is a field of engineering that deals with the study and application of electricity and electromagnetism. It is among the essential skill sets needed for an electric vehicle charging station installer company. An electrical engineer focuses on designing and planning electrical systems, analyzing system performance, and ensuring public safety when installing an EV charging station.

Electrical Safety

Electrical safety refers to the set of practices & procedures for ensuring the safety of personnel during the planning, installation, and operation of an electrical system. Electric vehicle charging station installer companies must adhere to and ensure protocols related to electrical safety. All employees and contractors working with electrical equipment must undergo safety training and follow safety guidelines to prevent accidents or other safety hazards.

Electrician

An electrician is a tradesperson who specializes in the installation, repair, and maintenance of electrical systems. An electrician is a crucial member of an electric vehicle charging station installer company, and their services are vital in planning, installing and testing the station's electrical grids.

Energy Management

Energy management refers to the practice of managing energy consumption in a building or facility. Electric vehicle charging station installers must be well-versed with energy management concepts like demand response and peak shaving as their charging station projects primarily focus on limiting the demand for power and optimizing energy efficiency.

Energy Storage

Energy Storage is the process of storing electrical energy generated from renewable energy sources, such as solar or wind, then using it when demanded. Installing energy storage systems is an essential part of electric vehicle charging station installation, which allows the operators to balance demand, reduce charging time, and ensure that energy is readily available when necessary.

Equipment Maintenance

Electric vehicle charging station installer companies must maintain and provide on-going equipment support, which includes periodic maintenance, troubleshooting, upgrading, and repair of electric vehicle charging stations. Proper maintenance, testing, and periodic upgrades are critical to the safe operation and long-term profitability of an electric vehicle charging station business.

Feasibility Study

A study conducted to evaluate whether a project is financially and technically feasible. When considering investing in an electric car charging station installer company, a feasibility study is essential to determine if the project will be profitable and if there is a demand for electric car charging stations in the targeted location. The study will evaluate factors such as the cost of installation, maintenance, and energy consumption, as well as potential partnerships and sales opportunities.

Financial Projections

Forecasts of a company's expected financial performance based on historical data and projected trends. In the case of an electric car charging station installer company, financial projections would include estimated revenue, expenses, and profits based on the number of charging stations installed and the expected usage rate over a specific period of time.

Fixed Costs

Expenses that do not change based on the number of charging stations installed or the level of usage. Examples of fixed costs for an electric car charging station installer company include lease payments for office space and salaries for administrative staff.

Franchise Agreement

A legal document that outlines the terms and conditions under which a company can use the brand name, trademarks, and business models of a larger corporation. When considering investing in an electric car charging station installer company, it is important to review the franchise agreement to ensure that it aligns with your goals and expectations. This agreement will outline requirements for investment, territory exclusivity, and ongoing fees for support and marketing. Make sure to review the agreement thoroughly and consult with a lawyer to ensure that you understand all of the terms before making a commitment.

Franchise Disclosure Document (FDD)

A legal document required by the Federal Trade Commission (FTC) that outlines the business opportunity being offered to prospective franchisees. The FDD includes information about the franchise system, the franchisor's history, fees and costs associated with the franchise, and other relevant details. It is important to carefully review the FDD before investing in an electric car charging station installer company to ensure that you understand all of the costs and requirements associated with the franchise.

Franchise Fee

A one-time fee paid by franchisees to the franchisor for the right to use the company's brand name and business model. In the case of an electric car charging station installer company, the franchise fee would cover the cost of training, support, and marketing materials provided by the franchisor. It is important to review the franchise agreement to determine the cost of the franchise fee and whether it is reasonable based on the benefits provided by the franchisor.

Franchisee

A business owner who purchases the rights to use a company's name, brand, and business model. In the case of an electric car charging station installer company, the franchisee would purchase the rights to use the company's brand name, marketing materials, and installation process. The franchisee assumes the risk of investment but benefits from the established reputation and support of the larger brand.

Franchisor

The parent company that grants the right to use its brand name, trademarks, and business model to franchisees. In the case of an electric car charging station installer company, the franchisor would be the company that provides the support, training, and marketing materials to franchisees.

Funding

The process of securing financial resources to invest in an electric car charging station installer company. There are several funding options available, including self-funding, bank loans, and venture capital. It is important to have a clear understanding of your investment needs and the potential return on investment before pursuing funding options. Research investment opportunities to ensure that they fit within your budget and align with your investment goals.

Future Growth Prospects

The potential for an electric car charging station installer company to expand and grow in the future. To evaluate future growth prospects, it is important to consider factors such as market demand, potential competitors, and the availability of resources such as funding and skilled labor.

Gateway

A gateway is a device that connects various charging stations to a central server. It is used to monitor and manage the charging stations from a single point. The gateway provides real-time data on the charging station's status, usage, and faults.

Geofencing

Geofencing refers to setting up virtual boundaries around the charging station's location. It is used to restrict the charging station's usage to only authorized vehicles within the specific area.

Government Incentives

Governments offer various incentives to encourage the installation of charging stations. These incentives may include tax credits, low-interest loans, and grants. It is essential to research the available incentives in the area where the charging station will be installed to maximize cost savings.

GPS Tracking

GPS tracking allows the monitoring of the charging station's location and usage in real-time. It provides valuable data on the usage patterns and enables effective maintenance scheduling.

Green Energy

Green energy refers to renewable energy sources such as wind, solar, and hydroelectric power. Investing in an electric car charging station installer company that sources green energy can be beneficial for the environment and also reduces operating costs due to lower electricity prices.

Grid Connection

A grid connection refers to the connection of the charging station with the electricity grid. A charging station must be connected to a grid for it to function correctly. It is important to know the capacity of the electricity grid in the area where the charging station will be installed.

Ground Proximity Detection

Ground proximity detection refers to the use of sensors to detect any object placed near the charging station. It is essential to avoid damaging the charging station due to accidental collisions. Proper ground proximity detection can also prevent tripping hazards for pedestrians and vehicles.

Grounding

Grounding refers to the process of connecting various parts of the charging station to a common ground point. Proper grounding is essential to avoid the risks of electric shock and fire hazards.

Growth Potential

The growth potential of an electric car charging station installer company is dependent on the increased demand for electric cars. It is important to research the growth potential of a company before investing.

Guaranteed Uptime

Guaranteed uptime refers to the percentage of time the charging station is operational without any downtime. A higher guaranteed uptime ensures that the charging station will be available to customers when needed, increasing customer satisfaction.

Hardware Maintenance Plan

A maintenance plan that ensures continued efficiency and effectiveness of the charging stations, including regular inspections, replacements, and repairs. It's important to understand the maintenance plan offered by the installer company to ensure long-term usage and reduced costs.

Hardware-to-installation ratio

The number of charging stations a company can install using a single hardware package. It's important to understand this ratio to ensure that the installer company can handle a large number of stations in one go without requiring additional hardware packages.

Heavy-Duty Charging

A charging system designed for heavy-duty vehicles, such as trucks or buses, that require higher charging capacities. It's important to understand if the installer company can handle heavy-duty charging installations, as it requires specialized knowledge and technology.

High-Voltage Charging

A charging system that uses higher power levels to shorten the charging time, commonly used for fast or rapid charging. It's important to understand if the installer company provides high-voltage charging options or not, as it will directly affect the charging time for vehicles.

Home Charging

A charging system designed for home or personal use, installed in residential buildings or garages. The installer company needs to be well-versed in home charging installations and understand the electricity supply for the residential building.

Host Site

The location where the charging station will be installed, such as a parking lot or a residential building. The host site is important to analyze the traffic volume, available facilities, and electricity supply to ensure efficient charging.

Host Site Agreement

An agreement signed between the charging station installer company and the host site owner that outlines the responsibilities of both parties concerning the installation, maintenance, and billing procedures. It's essential to have a clear agreement in place to avoid misunderstandings or disputes.

Hub and Spoke Network

A charging station network model where a central location serves as the primary hub, while the surrounding stations act as spokes. This network model ensures efficient electricity utilization and charging station usage.

Human Resource Training

The specific training and knowledge required for the employees of the installer company to install and maintain the charging stations. Proper training is required to ensure the charging stations operate efficiently and safely.

Hybridized Installations

The combination of public and private charging stations to create a network. By having hybridized installations, companies can have public access charging stations, as well as private ones for their employees or residents.

Incentives

Government or utility incentives that can offset costs for the installation of an electric car charging station, such as tax credits or rebates.

Industry Standards

Guidelines and recommendations established by industry organizations and regulatory bodies to ensure safety, performance, and quality in the installation and operation of electric car charging stations.

Infrastructure

The physical components required to install and operate an electric car charging station. This can include charging equipment, power supply, and communication systems.

Infrastructure Management

The ongoing maintenance, repair, and monitoring of the electric car charging station, including optimizing charging schedules and user data analysis.

Innovation

The development of new technologies, strategies, and designs that aim to improve the efficiency, performance, and user experience of electric car charging stations.

Installation Costs

The costs associated with the installation of an electric car charging station. This can include permits, equipment, and labor charges.

Installation Time

The amount of time required to install and commission an electric car charging station, including any testing and certification processes.

Integration

The process of ensuring compatibility between the electric car charging station and existing infrastructure, such as electrical systems and parking facilities.

Interoperability

The ability of electric car charging stations to operate with different types of electric vehicles and charging protocols, ensuring a seamless experience for users.

Investment Return

The expected financial returns on an investment in an electric car charging station installation company, taking into account factors such as installation costs, incentives, and market demand.

J1772 Adapter

An adapter used to connect the J1772 connector to a different type of charging station. It is important to ensure that the charging station installer company has experience working with J1772 adapters and can provide them if needed.

J1772 Compliance

The standard for electric vehicle charging connectors and stations in North America. It is important to ensure that the charging station installer company is familiar with J1772 compliance and can ensure that their installations meet these standards.

J1772 Connector

A standardized charging connector used in North America for electric vehicles. It is important to ensure that the charging station installer company is familiar with this connector and can provide it for their installations.

J1772 Receptacle

The part of a charging station that accepts the J1772 connector. It is important to ensure that the charging station installer company uses high-quality J1772 receptacles that can withstand frequent use and exposure to weather.

J1772 Socket

The socket on an electric vehicle designed to accept the J1772 connector. It is important to ensure that the charging station installer company has experience working with J1772 sockets and can properly install them.

Joule

The unit of energy used to measure how much electricity is consumed during charging. Before investing in a charging station installer company, it is important to understand the electricity usage and costs associated with charging.

Juicebox

A brand of electric car charging station that offers high-speed charging for electric vehicles. It is important to research different charging station brands to determine which one is the best fit for your needs.

Jumper Cable

A cable used to connect two different electrical systems. It is important to ensure that the charging station installer company has qualified personnel who can install jumper cables safely and correctly.

Jumper Kit

A kit used to connect an electric vehicle to a charging station. It is important to ensure that the charging station installer company has experience working with jumper kits and can properly install them.

Junction Box

A box that houses electrical connections and protects them from weather and other environmental factors. It is important to ensure that the charging station installer company chooses high-quality junction boxes that will protect the connections from damage.

Key Account Management (KAM)

A specialized customer service approach in which an account manager is assigned to provide dedicated support to a single or small group of high-value customers. Before investing in an electric car charging station installer company, it is important to understand their KAM strategy and the resources they allocate to key accounts, to ensure that your investment is protected and that your expectations are met.

Key Performance Indicators (KPIs)

Quantitative or qualitative measures that track progress toward specific business goals. Before investing in an electric car charging station installer company, it is important to understand their KPIs, such as customer satisfaction ratings, installation timelines, and revenue growth, to ensure that they align with your investment strategy.

Key Stakeholders

The individuals or groups that have a vested interest in the success or failure of an electric car charging station installer company, including investors, customers, employees, and regulators. Before investing in an electric car charging station installer company, it is important to understand the perspectives and needs of the key stakeholders, and to assess the company's ability to meet their expectations.

Kickback

A form of bribery in which a supplier or contractor offers to pay a percentage of their profits to an individual in exchange for favorable treatment. Before investing in an electric car charging station installer company, it is important to ensure that the company has ethical business practices in place and that their operations are transparent and above board.

Kilowatt Hours (kWh)

A measurement of the amount of energy transferred over time, typically used to calculate the cost of electric vehicle charging. Before investing in an electric car charging station installer company, it is important to understand how kWh measurements are used in billing and pricing structures, to ensure that your investment is financially viable and competitive.

Kiosk

A self-service, standalone structure used for public charging of electric vehicles. Investing in an electric car charging station installer company might involve exploring the kiosk market and understanding the different types of kiosks available, as well as their functionality, pricing, and mobility features.

Knock-Out Option

A clause in an investment agreement that allows the investor to cancel the investment based on certain predetermined conditions. Before investing in an electric car charging station installer company, it is important to understand the terms of the knock-out option and the circumstances under which it may be invoked, to protect yourself from potential losses.

Knowledge Base

A database that contains information about electric vehicle charging, including installation instructions, troubleshooting tips, and best practices. Before investing in an electric car charging station installer company, it is important to evaluate their knowledge base to ensure that they have the expertise necessary to meet your needs and provide support over the long term.

kWh Cost

The cost of one kilowatt hour of electricity. Before investing in an electric car charging station installer company, it is important to understand the kWh cost in your region and how it impacts the financial viability of your investment, particularly if your goal is to generate revenue from charging electric vehicles.

K-Whipped

A term used to describe electric vehicle drivers who are so reliant on public charging infrastructure that they purposely avoid charging at home. Before investing in an electric car charging station installer company, it is important to understand the degree to which their business strategy relies on customer behavior, and to assess whether it is sustainable and profitable over the long term.

LED lighting

Low-energy lighting technology commonly used in electric vehicle charging stations. LED lighting is energy-efficient and can be used to illuminate parking areas and charging stations.

Level 1 charging

A type of charging that uses a standard 120-volt AC outlet to charge an electric vehicle. Level 1 charging typically takes several hours to fully charge a vehicle, and is most commonly used at home or in workplaces where a vehicle is parked for an extended period of time.

Level 2 charging

A type of charging that uses a 240-volt AC electrical supply to charge an electric vehicle. Level 2 charging is faster than Level 1 and can typically fully charge a vehicle in a few hours. Level 2 charging is commonly used in public charging stations and in commercial settings.

Lifetime cost

The total cost of ownership of an electric vehicle charging station over its entire lifespan, including installation, maintenance, and energy bills. Calculating lifetime cost is an important factor to consider when deciding to invest in an electric vehicle charging station installer company.

Line voltage

The voltage supplied by the electric utility company to homes and businesses. Line voltage is typically 120 or 240-volts, and is used to power both Level 1 and Level 2 electric vehicle charging systems.

Lithium-ion battery

A type of battery commonly used in electric vehicles due to its high energy density and long lifespan. Lithium-ion batteries are known for their quick charging capabilities and ability to store large amounts of energy.

Load balancing

The process of distributing electrical load evenly among multiple charging stations to avoid failure due to overloading. Load balancing is important for electric car charging stations since it ensures that each station is functioning optimally and prevents damage to the charging network.

Load demand

The amount of electrical power required to charge electric vehicles in a specific area. Load demand is an important factor for electric vehicle charging station installers to consider when designing and installing charging infrastructure. Failure to calculate load demand accurately may lead to overloaded circuits and other issues.

Load management system

A software system used to manage and control the charging of electric vehicles. A load management system can optimize the use of energy and ensure that charging stations operate at optimal levels.

Local incentives

Incentives provided by local governments to encourage the use of electric vehicles and support the installation of charging stations. Local incentives may include tax credits, grants, or rebates for the installation of charging stations.

Maintenance and Support Services

A range of activities that the installed electric car charging station provider or repair professionals carry out to ensure the effectiveness and efficient operations of electric charging stations. Maintenance and support services may include monitoring power consumption, repairing technical issues, and providing customer support. Prioritizing maintenance and support services when selecting an installer company is essential to ensure the longevity of the charging station.

Management and Monitoring System

Platform used by charging station owners or operators to control, monitor, and manage the daily activities of the electric car charging stations. A comprehensive management and monitoring system should provide features like remote diagnostics, remote charging management, and support services. Management and Monitoring systems assist installer companies in ensuring efficient operations, and they can quickly address and fix any technical problems.

Mapping Software

Software utilized by electric car drivers to determine the nearest electric charging station, which charges the most affordable fees, and provides easy navigation from their current locations to the station. Mapping software is beneficial for electric car charging station installer companies because it enables them to reach a wider audience, better manage demand, and increases visibility.

Maximum Power Output

The maximum amount of energy an electric car charging station can provide at any given point. It is indicated in kilowatts and represents the maximum charging speed of the station. Knowing the maximum power output of a charging station is critical to ensure that it suits the needs of electric vehicle owners and can offer quick charging, which is essential in areas where there is high demand.

Megawatt-hour (MWh)

A unit of energy measurement used in the pricing and billing of electric car charging stations. It represents one million watt-hours or the amount of energy produced by one megawatt of electricity in an hour. Understanding how to calculate MWh is important in determining electric charging station costs because it measures the amount of electricity consumed by electric vehicles and how much energy the station requires to run.

Metering

A process of measuring the amount of energy that passes through an electric car charging station. Metering enables electric vehicle owners to be billed accurately for the amount of electricity they consume after charging their vehicles. Understanding the metering process is critical for installer companies to ensure they can manage power usage and accurately bill customers.

Mobile App

A software application that controls, manages and monitors the performance of electric car charging stations from a mobile device. Mobile apps can be utilized by charging station owners, operators, and customers to manage billing, track charging time, locate stations, and receive alerts on technical issues. It's a convenience feature that all installer companies should prioritize to improve the user experience and drive more demand.

Modularity

A characteristic that refers to the ability of an electric car charging station to adapt and grow with the increasing demand for charging services. It can be achieved through the use of expandable hardware, movable units, or adding more charging ports based on the demand. Modularity is a desirable feature to consider when installing an electric car charging station to guarantee its long-term viability and affordability.

Multi-Port Charger

A charging station that has two or more charging ports that enable multiple vehicles to charge simultaneously. Offering convenience, faster turnover, and reduced wait times, many electric car owners prefer to use multi-port chargers instead of single chargers. For commercial charging companies, multi-port chargers are advantageous because they permit them to increase efficiency and profits while reducing costs.

National Electrical Code (NEC)

A set of guidelines and standards developed by the National Fire Protection Association (NFPA) in the United States that outlines the minimum requirements for safe electrical installations. It is important for electric car charging station installer companies to adhere to NEC to ensure compliance and avoid fines or legal issues.

National Renewable Energy Laboratory (NREL)

A government-owned, contractor-operated research facility in the United States that focuses on energy efficiency and renewable energy technologies, including electric vehicle charging systems. NREL conducts research, development, and deployment activities to advance the industry and improve its technologies.

NEMA

Stands for National Electrical Manufacturers Association, a trade organization that represents American companies who manufacture electrical equipment, including electric vehicle charging stations. NEMA publishes technical specifications, standards, and guidelines for the industry.

Net Metering

A billing system used by utility companies that allows customers who generate their own electricity with solar or wind power systems to sell excess power back to the grid. This can be beneficial for electric car charging station installer companies who also have solar or wind power systems installed on their properties.

Networked Charging Stations

Electric vehicle charging stations that are connected together with a communication system, allowing for more efficient management and usage. They can be monitored and operated remotely, and data is collected to analyze usage patterns and adjust pricing.

Networking

The process of establishing and maintaining relationships with other individuals or companies in the electric car charging station installation industry to gain potential business referrals, partnerships, or collaborations. It can involve attending events, joining organizations, or connecting with individuals on social media platforms.

Networking Protocol

A set of rules and standards that governs how networked electric car charging stations communicate and exchange data with one another. Without consistent and standardized protocols, different charging station brands might not be able to communicate with one another, limiting the usefulness and effectiveness of networked charging stations.

New Technology

In the rapidly evolving electric car charging station installation industry, new technologies are constantly being developed and released. It is important for installer companies to stay up-to-date with new advances to remain competitive, offer the best products and services, and meet customer demands.

Non-demand Rates

This is a type of electricity rate offered by utility companies that does not take into account the amount of electricity a customer uses at any given time. Instead, customers are charged a flat rate based on their overall usage during the billing period. Non-demand rates can be more affordable for electric car charging station installer companies who have a consistent need for electricity.

Nonprofit Charging Station Installers

Nonprofit organizations are also entering the electric car charging station installation industry. These organizations may have specific goals or missions related to environmentalism or sustainability, and may offer unique perspectives and incentives for electric vehicle owners to choose their services. Nonprofit charging station installers can also apply for government grants or subsidies to expand their operations.

Onboard Charger

An onboard charger is a device in an EV that converts the AC power received from the charging station into DC power to charge the battery. The onboard charger determines the maximum charging rate for the battery and plays a crucial role in the speed of charging.

On-Site Assessment

An on-site assessment is an evaluation performed by an electric car charging station installer company to determine the best charging structure and location for a business. It includes an analysis of the available electrical infrastructure, site location, the type of EV charging station, and the level of charging that the business requires. This assessment helps the installer company provide an accurate estimate and plan for the installation.

Open Network

An open network refers to the ability of EV owners to use various public charging stations, regardless of which company operates them. Open networks offered by various EV charging companies allow users to access a wide range of charging stations with different pricing plans.

Operational Costs

Operational costs refer to the ongoing expenses associated with operating and maintaining the electric car charging station. These costs include electricity usage costs, repair and maintenance costs, and any fees associated with using third-party networks.

Operator

The operator of an electric car charging station is the entity responsible for the installation, operation, and maintenance of the station. It can be a manufacturer, utility company, or an independent provider. Before investing in an electric car charging station installer company, business owners must research the operator's reputation and experience in the market.

Outlet Capacity

Outlet capacity refers to the maximum amount of power that can be delivered to an EV from the electric car charging station. Outlet capacity can vary depending on the outlet type and the charging station's power rating, which can range from 3.7 kW to 350 kW. Businesses must consult with a professional EV charging station installer company to determine the outlet capacity ideal for their EV charging needs.

Outlet Compatibility

Outlet compatibility refers to the ability of the electric car charging station to support different EV plug types or adapter types based on the need of the EV drivers. This is especially important in a public charging station, where different EV models with different adapter types require charging.

Outlet Types

Outlet types refer to the different types of electric outlets that can be used for charging EVs. They include Level 1, Level 2, and DC fast charging outlets, each with its unique charging time and capability.

Overload Protection

Overload protection is a feature of electric car charging stations that prevents the electrical wiring from being overloaded by too much current being drawn at once. This feature is critical to the safety of the charging station, as it minimizes the risk of electrical fires and other hazards.

Ownership Options

This refers to the various models that businesses can choose from when investing in an electric car charging station installer company. These models include ownership of the charging stations, leasing the charging stations, and financing options. Each of these options comes with its advantages and disadvantages. Business owners must consider their budget, needs, and long-term goals when choosing an ownership option.

Partnership

Choosing the right electric car charging station installer company means finding a partner that can help guide you through the installation process and address any future maintenance and support needs. It's important to choose a company that values transparency and collaboration, especially when it comes to budgeting and timelines.

Payment Methods

Payment methods are an essential factor to consider before investing in an electric car charging station installer company. Offering multiple payment methods like credit card, RFID, mobile app, or other electronic payment methods makes it easier for drivers and station operators to manage transactions. Having a clear and reliable payment system can also help in proper billing, revenue tracking, and analysis.

Permits

Permits are necessary for the installation of EV charging stations, and they may vary based on the location and type of installation. In some cases, permits may be required from the local government, the utility company, or both. These permits not only ensure that the installation meets safety standards but also help to prevent future legal issues and penalties.

Plug Types

Electric car charging stations support various plug types, such as CCS, CHAdeMO, and Type 2. The type of plug required depends on the car model and manufacturer. Before investing in a charging station installer company, it's essential to ensure the chosen station is compatible with most electric car models and has the right number and types of plugs installed.

Power Management System

The Power Management System is an essential part of an electric car charging station that helps manage power usage, costs, and safety aspects. Before investing in a charging station installer company, it is crucial to evaluate the Power Management System's features and functionalities. A good power management system will prevent power overloads or failure, optimize power usage, and reduce electricity costs.

Power Supply

The power supply is an essential factor to consider before investing in an electric car charging station installer company. Each station requires a specific amount of power that can vary between stations, which is why it's crucial to evaluate the available power supply and potential upgrades or modifications. In some cases, installing additional infrastructure or upgrading the transformer may be necessary to ensure that the charging station works effectively.

Preventative Maintenance

A charging station's durability and peak performance depend on proper maintenance and upkeep. Thus, it's essential to choose an electric car charging station installer company that offers regular preventive maintenance plans. Preventative maintenance involves routine checking and servicing of equipment, identifying potential issues, and corrective actions to ensure smooth operations and better user experience.

Pricing Models

Understanding the pricing models for electric car charging stations is crucial before investing in a charging station installer company. Charging stations typically have three pricing models

Professional Installation

It is critical to choose an electric car charging station installer company that offers professional installation. Station installation requires expert technicians who have experience with electrical wiring, permits, and related safety requirements. Professional installation ensures safety and longevity for the charging station.

Public vs. Private

Before investing in an electric car charging station installer company, it's important to decide whether to install public or private EV charging stations. Public stations are installed in public areas like streets, parking lots, or highways, while private stations get installed in residential complexes or company premises. Choosing the right type of charging stations requires considering factors like location, charging speed, and accessibility.

Range anxiety

Refers to the fear of running out of power while driving an electric car. Range anxiety is a particular concern for electric car owners and affects the adoption of EVs. Installing charging stations in strategic locations and properly advertising their availability helps alleviate range anxiety, enabling more people to purchase electric vehicles, thus contributing to a growing market and potential customers for the electric car charging station installer company.

Redundancy

Refers to the deployment of backup charging equipment, especially in high-traffic areas or in commercial applications. Deploying redundant charging equipment ensures a seamless charging experience for electric car owners, avoids charging station downtime, and helps prevent lost revenue for the owners of the charging station installer company. Deploying redundant charging equipment also mitigates the risk of power outages or other technical problems.

Regional regulations

Refers to the specific rules and regulations that vary from one geographic location to another. Some countries and even some states have unique regulations and compliance requirements that govern the installation and operation of electric car charging stations. The electric car charging station installer company must be familiar with the relevant regulations and must ensure that all their installations comply with them.

Remote monitoring

Refers to the ability to monitor the status of charging stations remotely using real-time data, analytics, and predictive maintenance tools. Remote monitoring helps ensure that charging stations are operating smoothly and optimally, reducing downtime and maintaining optimal uptime levels. Remote monitoring enables the electric car charging station installer company to identify potential problems before they occur, enabling remote diagnosis and repair.

Renewable energy credits

Refers to the incentives and credits that governments and utility providers offer for investing in renewable energy sources. Electric car charging stations can be powered by renewable sources, and owners of the charging stations are often eligible for these credits. Renewable energy credits enable owners of electric car charging stations to lower their electricity costs, hence increasing profitability and reducing carbon footprint.

Retrofitting

Refers to the process of modifying existing structures or equipment to accommodate the installation of an electric car charging station. Retrofitting measures may vary depending on the current infrastructure and electrical capacity of the building. This process may require additional wiring or the installation of new electrical panels to handle the load of the charging station. Proper planning and evaluation of the charging station's electrical requirements are crucial during the retrofitting process to ensure safety and optimum performance.

Return on Investment (ROI)

Refers to the measure of profitability of the charging station installation for the investors. ROI is a critical performance metric for evaluating the success of the electric car charging station installer company's business model. ROI can vary depending on the location, charging station utilization rate, and maintenance costs. The actual deployment and investment in charging stations should carefully consider the projected ROI.

Revenue per station

Refers to the average amount of revenue a single charging station generates for the owners of the electric car charging station installer company. This is an important metric when scaling up an electric car charging station installation company's operations. As the number of installed charging stations grows, measuring the revenue per station helps owners determine expanding or contracting specific locations, identify areas with higher earning potential, and avoid unprofitable investments.

Revenue-sharing

Refers to the business model where the owners of the electric car charging station installer company and the location owners of the charging stations share the profits from the station's usage. This model incentivizes owners of the installation company to select high-traffic areas and deploy the most efficient charging stations to generate the most revenue. In return, owners of the location of the charging stations can turn these stations into a passive source of revenue, allowing them to entice customers to visit their premises or place of business.

Robustness testing

Refers to the process of testing and evaluating the durability and longevity of charging stations to withstand unforeseen mechanical or environmental challenges. Robustness testing helps the electric car charging station installer company in identifying the weak points of their charging stations and taking proactive steps to ensure the stations remain operational and reliable over the long term. Proper robustness testing ensures that charging stations deliver maximum uptime and return on investment.

Safety Regulations

Compliance with National Electrical Code (NEC), Occupational Safety and Health (OSHA), and local building code regulations. The installation of electric car charging stations must comply with these regulations and standards for user safety and liability protection.

Scalability

The ability of the installer company to adapt to changing demands for electric vehicle charging stations. Scalability includes the ability to expand operations, manage multiple sites, and adding new services or products to the portfolio.

Service and Maintenance

The installer company must have a service and maintenance plan in place to ensure the charging stations are kept in good condition, perform optimally, and operational. The plan includes periodical inspections, repairs, and replacement of damaged parts to ensure the charging stations are available for customers 24/7.

Service Level Agreement

A contract between the electric car charging station installer company and the customer. It outlines the scope of work, supports and services, installation timelines, and terms and conditions. A detailed service-level agreement helps in avoiding any misunderstandings between the parties.

Site Assessment

A process of analyzing the site location where the electric car charging station is to be installed. It assesses the location's electrical infrastructure, usage, accessibility, and the number of potential users. Site assessment helps in determining the feasibility of installing an electric car charging station and is crucial in identifying the installation costs.

Smart Charging Technology

Advanced charging technology that helps in the efficient management of charging stations, including load balancing, energy demand, and power distribution. Smart charging technology enables time-of-use charging, supports remote monitoring, and enables users to manage their charging preferences and payment options.

Software Platforms

Electric car charging station software platforms help in managing the charging stations, user accounts, payments, and technical support. They provide a user-friendly interface for customers to manage their charging activities seamlessly.

Staff Training

Installer companies must invest in staff training to ensure they are up-to-date with the latest electric vehicle technology, charging equipment, and regulations. Having well-trained staff helps in providing high-quality installation services, maintenance, and technical support for electric vehicle charging stations.

Sustainability

Electric car charging station installer companies must have strategies in place to reduce environmental impact, save energy, and promote sustainable practices. This includes sourcing materials responsibly, reducing waste and emissions, and promoting efficient energy usage.

Technical Expertise

Technical expertise refers to the knowledge and skills required to assemble and install an electric charging station. The installer must have extensive knowledge of the electrical aspects involved, including proper grounding and electrical lines' right placement. They should also have knowledge of refrigeration, electrical permits, and local codes to ensure the installation of a safe and efficient charging station. The installer should have appropriate training and a track record of knowledge and experience in the industry.

Technologies for Smart Charging

Smart charging is an intelligent technology that uses communication between the charger and the vehicle to optimize energy use, minimize charging costs, and avoid overloading power grids. Several Technologies for Smart Charging exists, such as vehicle-to-grid (V2G), the Internet of Things (IoT) based infrastructure, etc., to help operators control energy demand and provide a greener solution of charging with minimized environmental impact.

Technology Compatibility

This term refers to the ability of the charging station installer to provide equipment that is compatible with the technology used in electric vehicles. It requires knowledge of the type of charging port used by each model, as well as understanding the user interface of the station. Consideration must be taken in making sure that the charging station meets the specifications of the electric vehicle and its charging protocol. Compatibility is essential for ensuring the safe and efficient transfer of power from the charging station to the vehicle's battery.

Tesla Destination Charging

Tesla Destination Charging, established by Tesla Motors, is a network of charging stations in social and shopping centers, restaurants, and hotels around the world. Tesla offers businesses the opportunity to install and maintain Tesla wall connectors as a way to attract more customers and promote electric vehicle stations. This partnership's benefits include providing the necessary technical, marketing, and operational assistance to deploy the Tesla charging station in recognized locations.

Third-Party Provider

Third-party providers offer an innovative solution to electric vehicle charging by constructing and maintaining charging stations available to clients at a known usage cost. The third-party provider will provide maintenance, billing, customer service, and all necessary technical support associated with modern energy management. Having a third-party provider reduces a lot of the burden of EV charger ownership, and businesses benefit by giving customers an easy-to-use alternative to traditional fuel.

Tiered Pricing

This term refers to an electric charging system where the supplier charges for services defined by a pre-established scheme. The pricing system measures the energy consumed, charging station size, and other variables to determine the tariff rate for the service. Tiered pricing can offer customers more control over their costs, and suppliers can customize their offering to expand their market share.

Time to Charge

This term is the estimated amount of time it will take an electric vehicle to charge based on the charger's output and the vehicle's battery size. Different types of charging stations provide different rates and outputs of charge. Fast chargers are an expensive solution, but they deliver high speeds and shorten the time required to charge a vehicle. Time to charge relates to adoption of the typical charge session and the driver's preference for a fast, efficient charging experience.

Time-of-Use Rates

Time-of-use rates refer to the pricing structure that varies depending on the time of the day or week when the charging station is in use. The demand for power mains fluctuates by the time of day, and the pricing system reflects this. Providers will charge different fees based on the time of day, with higher rates applied to peak periods to limit the load on the network.

Trade-In Program

A trade-in program relates to an initiative in which an electric charger installer company shows a willingness to offer discounts on the return of a used unit while you acquire a newer station. For instance, should an electric vehicle owner have a less advanced charging station, they may find it beneficial to trade it in for a newer, more advanced model with a unified interface with their car model. The trade-in program facilities updating and replacing outdated equipment, providing incentives for businesses and private owners to install modern and efficient charging stations.

Transportable Charger

The transportable charger refers to a commercial electric vehicle charger that can be moved from one location to another. The charging station will be portable, and businesses can move the charger to places where there is no power supply, providing users with quality electric vehicle charging capabilities. This possibility offers greater flexibility than more traditional charging station models and steps up the level of accessibility to electric vehicles charging.

Underlying Technology

Underlying technology refers to the hardware and software used to power and manage the electric car charging station. It is important to invest in a company that uses reliable and up-to-date technology to ensure a smooth and efficient user experience.

Uninterrupted Power Supply

An uninterrupted power supply is essential for the smooth operation of the electric car charging station. It ensures that charging is not interrupted due to power outages or other issues. It is important to invest in a company that offers uninterrupted power supply to ensure a positive user experience.

Universal Compatibility

Universal compatibility refers to the ability of the electric car charging station to charge all types of electric vehicles, regardless of their make or model. It is important to invest in a company that offers universal compatibility to maximize the potential customer base.

Upfront Costs

Upfront costs refer to the initial expenses associated with installing an electric car charging station. This includes the cost of the charging equipment, installation, permits and inspections, and any necessary electric upgrades. It is important to factor in upfront costs when considering investing in an electric car charging station installer company.

Upkeep and Maintenance

Upkeep and maintenance refer to the ongoing costs associated with keeping the electric car charging station operational. This includes routine maintenance, repairs, and upgrades. It is important to invest in a company that offers reliable upkeep and maintenance services.

Usage Rates

Usage rates refer to the fees charged to customers for using the electric car charging station. It is important to invest in a company that offers competitive usage rates to attract and retain customers.

User Data

User data refers to the information collected by the electric car charging station installer company about the usage patterns of the station. This data can be valuable for optimizing the charging station's performance and improving the user experience. It is important to invest in a company that collects and uses user data responsibly.

User Experience

User experience refers to the ease and convenience of using the electric car charging station. It is important to invest in a company that prioritizes user experience by providing easy-to-use stations, clear directions, and reliable customer service.

User Safety

User safety is a top priority when investing in an electric car charging station installer company. It is important to invest in a company that prioritizes user safety by adhering to safety standards, installing high-quality equipment, and providing adequate training to users.

Utility Company

A utility company is responsible for providing electricity to power the electric car charging station. It is important to research the utility company's reliability and capacity before investing in an electric car charging station installer company. The capacity of the utility company will determine how many charging stations can be installed and how fast they can be charged.

Vehicle Compatibility

Vehicle compatibility means the type of electric vehicles that can be charged on a particular charging station. Some stations are only compatible with specific electric vehicle models or manufacturers, while others may be universal. Before investing in an electric car charging station installer company, make sure to check if their charging stations support the compatibility of your electric vehicle.

Vendor Experience

Vendor experience refers to the length of time an electric car charging station installer company has been in business. A company with a longer track record has more experience and knowledge about the electric vehicle industry, which can result in a more efficient installation process.

Vendor Services

Vendor services refer to the various services provided by an electric car charging station installer company, including installation, maintenance, and repair services. Choosing a vendor that provides excellent services can help you save money and time in the long run.

Ventilation

Ventilation refers to the air circulation system in the charging station's location. A well-ventilated charging station allows air to flow freely, which aids in regulating the temperature and preventing overheating during the charging process. A charging station without proper ventilation carries a higher risk of damage to the charging station and the vehicle.

Vibration Resistance

Vibration resistance is one of the requirements for an electric car charging station as it reduces the likelihood of damage or disconnection of power supply when subjected to continuous vibrations from motor vehicles. The charging station should be durable enough to withstand unpredictable vibrations and still function properly.

Voltage

Voltage is the amount of electric energy that is supplied by an electric car charging station installer company. The voltage requirement for an electric car may vary based on the make and model of the car. A higher voltage means faster charging and vice versa. Understanding the voltage requirement is crucial for choosing an appropriate charging station installer company that meets your needs.

Voltage Drop

Voltage drop refers to the reduction in voltage due to a long charging cable or inadequate wire thickness. A high voltage drop leads to slow charging, reducing the efficiency of the charging process. A professional electric car charging station installer company must evaluate and optimize the charging station's electrical system and cable length to achieve a minimum voltage drop.

Voltage Regulator

A voltage regulator is a critical component in an electric car charging station that regulates the voltage of the charging station. A voltage regulator ensures that the charging station supplies a constant voltage to the electric vehicle during the charging process, which prevents overcharging and maximizes battery life.

Voltage Stabilizer

A voltage stabilizer is an equipment used to regulate and stabilize unstable voltage fluctuations in the power grid. The voltage stabilizer protects charging stations from damage that can be caused by voltage fluctuations due to sudden power surges or outages.

Volume

Volume refers to the capacity of the charging station. For instance, a charging station that can charge a single electric vehicle at a time will have a lower volume compared to a charging station with multiple charging points. Larger charging stations can cater to more electric vehicles at a time, making them more efficient in handling high volumes of electric vehicles.

Wallbox

A wallbox charging station is a popular option for home charging, as it provides a convenient and safe method of charging electric vehicles. Before investing, ensure the installer company offers wallbox options that suit your specific requirements.

Warranty

It's essential to know the warranty offered by an installer company before investing in an electric car charging station. A reliable warranty ensures that the charging station stands the test of time and potential defects are addressed. A warranty typically covers replacement or repair of faulty charging stations, helping to reduce your financial burden should any issues arise.

Wattage

The total amount of power consumed by an electric car charging station determines its wattage. Before investing in an installer company, it is essential to know the wattage of the charging stations they offer. A higher wattage charging station can charge vehicles faster than a lower wattage station, making it a critical consideration for commercial facilities where time is of the essence.

Weatherproofing

Proper weatherproofing of electric car charging stations is vital to ensure they can withstand harsh environmental conditions. It's important to ensure that the installer company uses high-quality weatherproofing materials and techniques to protect your charging stations from moisture, UV rays, and other factors that may cause damage.

Wireless Charging

Wireless charging is a modern and innovative technology that eliminates the need for cords or cables, making it a convenient option for electric car charging. However, the technology is relatively new and can come at a higher cost. Before investing, be sure to weigh the pros and cons of wireless charging and ensure that the installer company provides reliable wireless charging options.

Wiring

The wiring of an electric car charging station is a crucial aspect that requires careful consideration. A proper wiring setup ensures that electricity flows efficiently to the charging station, ensuring maximum performance. Before investing, it's important to ensure that the installer company takes proper precautions when setting up the wiring to avoid electrical hazards, system failures, and other issues that can cause your investment to fall short.

Workplace Charging

Workplace charging stations are becoming prevalent in commercial facilities to facilitate employee and customer electric vehicle charging. Before investing, it's essential to ensure that the installer company offers workplace charging options that are tailored to suit your specific needs.

Yard Management System

A software platform used to track and manage the movement of vehicles in a particular area, such as a shipping yard or parking lot. While not directly related to charging station installation, installers may work closely with companies that use this type of system to ensure that their charging stations are integrated properly.

Y-connect Terminal

A type of connector used to join two or more wires together. This can be particularly useful in the installation of charging stations, where multiple wires may need to be joined together to ensure proper electrical flow.

Y-connector Cable

A type of cable used to connect two charging stations together, allowing them to share a power source. This can be particularly useful in areas with high traffic, as it allows more vehicles to be charged at once.

Yellow Light of Doom

A warning light on electric vehicle charging stations that indicates an error or problem with the system. This can include everything from a power outage to a wiring issue, and it's important for charging station installers to be able to quickly identify and fix the problem.

Yes Energy Management

A platform used to remotely monitor and manage electric vehicle charging stations. This system allows companies to track usage, collect payment, and even prioritize charging during peak times to ensure every car gets the power it needs.

Y-harness Cable

A type of cable used to connect multiple charging stations to a single power source. This can help reduce installation costs, as fewer electrical lines need to be run to each individual charging station.

Yield Curve

A graph that shows the relationship between the interest rates on bonds of different maturities. Charging station installer companies may use this data to make decisions about the pricing of their charging services, as well as the types of equipment they invest in.

Yield Management

A strategy used by charging station installer companies to maximize profits by adjusting pricing based on demand, time of day, and other factors. This helps them ensure they are making the most money possible while still making their charging stations affordable for consumers.

YouTube Channel

A social media platform that allows companies to share educational content and tips related to their operation. Electric vehicle charging station installer companies may use this platform to build their brand and increase awareness of their services.

Yunnan Baiyao

A type of traditional Chinese medicine that has been used for centuries to support wound healing and reduce inflammation. While not directly related to electric vehicle charging station installation, it's important for installers to prioritize their own physical wellbeing to ensure they can perform their work to the best of their abilities.